BLACK MEN
in White Coats:

100 RULES FOR SUCCESS!

BLACK MEN
in White Coats:

100 RULES FOR SUCCESS!

DALE OKORODUDU, MD

Black Men In White Coats: 100 Rules for Success!

©2019 by Dale Okorodudu

Published by BMWC Media, Dallas, Texas

Join Our Online Community of Diverse Premeds, Medical Students, & Doctors at:

www.DiverseMedicine.com

Make sure you do this!

This book is dedicated to my big brother in a white coat!

Daniel Okorodudu, MD
Thank you for mentoring me and running with all my crazy ideas over the years. I love you, bro!

CONTENTS

INTRODUCTION

DR. DALE OKORODUDU

Founder of Black Men in White Coats
Specialty: Pulmonary &
Critical Care Medicine

READY FOR TAKEOFF

The plane flight that would spark a generation of marginalized youth to pursue greatness took off from St. Louis, Missouri, one cold fall night. At the time, I was a junior in college and was headed home to see my family. Dressed like many other black men of my generation, I stepped onto the plane wearing baggy sweat pants and a hoody. After grabbing my seat and making myself comfortable, a middle age woman squeezed into the seat next to me. That simple decision, her choice of seat, changed my life forever.

What does it take to give a person purpose? What does it take to set a man on a mission? For me, it was a two-hour plane trip from St. Louis to Houston, Texas. You may be thinking that this kind woman had a heartfelt story that motivated me to be great. If so, you're absolutely wrong. What she did have were choice words and opinions. Mind you, we had never met prior to this flight, yet she deemed it appropriate to verbally assault my morale for two hours. As I recall, some of her key questions were:

Why do you dress like that? Don't you have clothes that fit you?

Why do you talk like that? You talk funny. Do you think you're cool or something?

Do you think anybody will ever take you seriously? They won't. You're not going to be successful!

Little did this woman know she was sitting next to a straight 'A' student. She had no clue that she was speaking with a future medical doctor. Never in her wildest dreams would she have believed that this young man, who she had belittled for two hours, would spark a fire that would ignite the hearts and minds of so many black boys and men with hopes and dreams of success! Never would she have envisioned the *Black Men in White Coats* movement! But should she somehow get a hold of this book today, I'd like to say, thank you.

Thank you for helping me realize what some (not most) people think when they see individuals who look like me. Thank you for inspiring me to change the narrative for young black men in America. Thank you for giving me the fuel to make sure other black men aren't made to feel small the same way you attempted to make me feel that cold evening. Thank you.

AN ENDANGERED SPECIES

One day I read a news article that said the already low number of black men applying to medical school was on the decline. I was dumbfounded. According to the article, the number had actually been higher 30 years prior. CRAZY! Reflecting on my airplane incident, I knew I had to do something about this, but I wasn't quite sure what that would be.

I called my brother, who was in his fellowship training at Duke, and one of my buddies, Simon, who was a medical student there. After telling them about this alarming report, I asked if they'd join me for a roundtable discussion focused on why less black men were applying to medical school. Gladly, they both agreed, and we met in the game room of Daniel's apartment complex. I set up my cell phone and we recorded the first ever "Black Men in White Coats" video. I made up that name because I wanted to highlight the contrast between black and white.

My buddy Adeleke posted the video on his YouTube channel. I remember him contacting me in excitement saying, "Dale, your video is going to go viral, the counts keep going up!" Sure enough, he was right, and since then (2013) we have had multiple videos and posts about our work go viral! I don't say this to brag, but to emphasize a single point: people want to see more black men in white coats! That was my sign to keep on pushing for this mission.

WHY I WROTE THIS BOOK

Simply put, I am a leadership junkie and came to realize that in order to be one of the few Black Men in White Coats, you had to have learned a few success rules along the way. With the already low numbers of black men applying to medical school declining, I knew that the ones who made it had something important to share.

So, I decided to launch a podcast which I called . . . you guessed it, Black Men in White Coats. On my show, I give black male clinicians a platform to share their struggles and successes. Week by week, I listened to some of the most inspiring messages and rules of success that I'd ever heard. Story after story, they defied the odds. Finally, it hit me. I had to write this book and share their wisdom. Not just for black men, but for everyone.

HOW TO READ THIS BOOK

If you read this book like I tell you to, I truly believe you'll be more successful in life. This is NOT a novel, so do NOT read it like one. I have written this book in a special way to make you reflect on each rule for success. It is important that you take the time to digest the information and answer the questions. This will help increase your awareness, which in turn will help you direct your own success. No matter your stage of life, there is something on these pages that can help you.

Here's how to read this book:

1) **Find a partner to read it with.**

Learning with an accountability buddy will push you to stay on track. You'll be surprised how much more growth you'll have when you discuss the topics with a partner compared to reading alone.

2) **Read only ONE rule per day.**

It's not a race. Take your time and meditate on each rule. Success doesn't happen over night. If you read one rule a day, you'll be done with this book in a little over three months, which is adequate time to truly study each lesson.

3) **Reflect and take action.**

Each rule is associated with at least one question. I have written these questions to encourage self-reflection in order to help you grow and have a true transformative experience. Challenge yourself to take action with each rule. If you do this, you'll see results!

Please keep in mind that this book was made from various podcast episodes. Each section starts with a rule followed by my brief introduction to that rule written in italics. Following my introduction, you'll read excerpts from my podcast guests. Because these are quoted excerpts, there will be grammatical errors as the podcast was not intended to be a work of literary art. The words are written in the same format that they were freely spoken. I have only altered the text minimally in order to keep the truest essence of each doctor's story. As you read through each section, imagine the doctor is sitting there in the room with you.

I pray that the wisdom in this book can be used to propel you to new levels of success, servitude, and love. Let the transformation begin. Enjoy!

ACKNOWLEDGEMENTS

I'd like to acknowledge the 20 doctors featured in this book. When I began the *Black Men in White Coats* podcast, these individuals were the first to volunteer their time without reluctance. All I had to do was ask, and they were more than happy to participate. As you can imagine, anytime you are starting something new, many people are skeptical or don't want to offer support for various reasons. Making change isn't easy, and in order to do so, you need individuals like these 20 who can see your vision and get behind it to support the desired outcome. So, to the docs in this book, THANK YOU!

DR. MICHAEL KELSO

Specialty:
Gastroenterology

RULE # 1: DO 'YOU' AND LIVE TO YOUR FULL POTENTIAL.

You're not competing with anyone but yourself. When you try to fit in with others rather than living to your full potential, you make your life so much harder. Just do 'you'!

I moved to Baltimore in 1996 when my Dad told us he needed to try to get a job somewhere else, and we could no longer afford living in the area that we were living. Also, job opportunities in Baltimore seemed more appealing, and we'd be closer to family. So, I went from a pretty diverse suburban neighborhood in Grand Prairie, Texas, to Baltimore, where I went into high school.

The high school was probably 95 percent African American, which was a huge shock for me. I'd never been in an environment like that. The city was rough. I felt out of place most of the time that I was there.

In the ninth grade, I remember trying to fit in by skipping classes and not doing my work. I nearly had to go to summer school for an English class that I had essentially failed, but was able to do makeup work to pass the class with a 'C.' I told myself that I would never allow myself to struggle like that again, or not to live to my full potential.

QUESTION: *What is one area of your life in which you are putting on a façade for others and not being your true self? What would your life look like if you could just be yourself in that area?*

RULE #2: SOMETIMES YOU HAVE TO TAKE RISKS.

It's easy for us to get comfortable where we are. Dr. Kelso sacrificed so much to get a research position at Johns Hopkins University, one of the world's best medical institutions. But when he realized that he was not fulfilled in that position, he knew he had to take a gamble.

I told my boss at Hopkins that I was not going to be able to fulfill my two-year commitment in the lab. Instead, I moved to North Carolina to establish my residency so I could be an in-state resident when I applied for medical school. That would make the odds of getting in a little easier, but also to apply for the Medical Education Program (MED), which is an intensive premed, pre-dental summer course. He sat me in his office and said: You know, I understand why you're leaving. Now, either you can gamble your life and win big or not gamble at all and neither win nor lose. That being said, I left the lab. That was in the summer of 2005. I packed everything up in my car, moved to North Carolina, with no job and no source of income. I spent the next two and a half months sleeping on the floor of an empty apartment of a friend of mine who had already moved out but still had a couple of months left on her lease.

QUESTION: *What risk do you need to take in order for you to make your dream become reality?*

RULE # 3: FIND A SPONSOR.

*A sponsor is a person who risks something that is important
to them so they can help you. For example, they might
risk their reputation by telling other people you are great
and that they should take a chance on you. Or, they might
risk their own money by paying something for you. The
important thing to know about getting a sponsor is that you
must earn their confidence in you. They'll only sponsor you
if they believe you can be successful.*

I applied for the MED program that spring and again, initially, I was rejected because my undergraduate Grade Point Average wasn't that great. Fortunately, a family friend who worked in the office had their program director take a look at my application, and I was able to get in. When I did the program, I decided that I was going to put my whole heart into it, and I was going to work hard as possible. I was going to do hard work and focus so much on it because I wanted to prove to myself and to everyone else that I could excel.

I finished the program in the top three of my MED class. I applied to medical school that same year. The program director, Mr. Larry Keith, was battling colon cancer and was in and out of the office. He mustered up enough energy to come in and sit on the admission board to make sure particular people were being strongly considered for admission to the medical school. I called the admissions office over and over again, asking whether my application had been reviewed. At one point, they told me that my application was not going to be considered for admission, and I wasn't even going to get an interview. My heart sank. If it wasn't for Mr. Keith sitting on the admission board and advocating strongly for me, I would have never gotten an interview. I would never have gotten the full scholarship to the University of North Carolina Medical School.

QUESTION: *Do you have a sponsor who will help you get to the next level? If not, what is your plan to earn the confidence of one?*

RULE #4: BE OPEN-MINDED.

You never know what you'll get out of an experience.
Dr. Kelso went on a trip to Africa to teach children and came back wanting to be a doctor.

Ultimately, I ended up graduating with a biology degree, still not knowing exactly what I wanted to do. I ended up traveling to Malawi in Africa for about a month and a half to teach HIV/AIDS education to children in rural primary schools. There, I became very aware of my own ambition to help people on a more personal level. To be able to touch the human body and address needs more pressing than your day to day preoccupations like paying bills, cell phones, or recreation activities, felt real to me.

I saw the gap in the health care provided there and the knowledge that children and their parents had about health conditions. I left there determined that I needed to be a clinician.

QUESTION: *What is one thing which you have been close-*

minded about? What is keeping you from being open-minded about it?

RULE #5: BELIEVE IN YOURSELF.

Many of us deal with Imposter Syndrome (a false sense of unworthiness even though you are qualified) and lose confidence in ourselves. To be successful as a doctor or in any profession, you must believe in yourself.

My advice is to surround yourself with individuals who want to see you succeed, and believe in yourself. Never ever give up, work hard, believe in yourself and it's possible. It's possible for you to live out your dream, whether it's to be a doctor, whether it's to be a nurse—whatever profession you want to go into, it's possible.

QUESTION: *On a scale of 0–10, with 0 being not confident and 10 being extremely confident, how confident are you that you can achieve your goals? Why did you select that number?*

NOTES

_____

_____

_____

_____

_____

_____

_____

_____

_____

_____

_____

_____

_____

_____

_____

_____

_____

_____

_____

_____

_____

_____

DR. LAMAR HASBROUCK

Specialty:
Internal Medicine

RULE #1: BE DRIVEN BY YOUR DEFICITS.

Don't use them as excuses. Dr. Hasbrouck defines his upbringing as one full of many deficits. Whereas many people would use this as an excuse, he chose to use it as motivation. It was a deficit in healthcare within his community that led him to become a medical doctor.

The other deficit in my community was a deficit in terms of health and healthcare—especially in terms of wellness care, or what we might call preventive care. Myself and my three siblings never went to the to the doctor's office when we were feeling well. We went when we broke something or busted something or needed stitches or had a high fever, and it was typically through the urgent care or the emergency department. Dental care was not heard of; there were no preventive dental exams. I recall that my preventive care for dentistry was when the Crest Mobile Unit came and parked in my community and handed out free toothbrushes, little small tubes of toothpaste and those little red tablets that you could chew to find where you had cavities. That was my dental care growing up—a lot of deficits.

When I got to college and realized this, I decided that if I finished college, I would be a health professional so I could help address communities with similar deficits.

QUESTION: *What is one excuse that has been holding you back? What would happen if you used that excuse as a motivator instead?*

RULE #2: EMBRACE THE CHALLENGE.

A common theme for many of my podcast guests
was someone telling them that they wouldn't be successful.
It even happened to me. Rather than running from it, many
of us embraced the challenge.

I decided I was going to be a doctor my freshman year. The problem was, my counselor, who happened to be an African American man, did everything he could to discourage me. Essentially, he told me, "It's going to be tough. You got to have good grades and compete with a lot of other people, and they don't take everybody." This was my first or second week on campus! He didn't know me from a can of paint, nor did he know my potential. Admittedly, I was in over my head, but he didn't know that. Ultimately, I decided to pursue medicine because many people, starting with my assigned counselor at the University of California, Berkeley, decided for me that I couldn't.

It was about pushing myself and challenging myself to do something everyone said I couldn't. I didn't know how I would do it, but I felt that I could harness the environment and find what I needed to learn in order to become a physician. By setting that audacious goal and achieving it, I knew I could help communities much like the one that I grew up in with many of those deficits.

QUESTION: *What is one challenge that you have been avoiding? Why are you avoiding it?*

RULE #3: GET HELP.

Becoming a doctor isn't easy. If it was, everyone would do it. When times get tough, any one of us can breakdown. If that happens, you must get help!

My greatest challenge was my first year in residency as an intern, being assigned to the medical ward. I automatically went from being a medical student, to orientation, to becoming a physician.

As a first-year physician, I was an intern who oversaw a service with 13-15 patients in it. Trying to get to know those patients, plus getting through the daily rounding, daily errands, all the assignments from X-Rays to CT-scans to chasing down labs, and writing progress notes—it was very, very overwhelming.

I finally hit my breakpoint on rounds one morning. My eyes glazed over. I felt like I was out of control. I was overwhelmed, out of my depth and knew that something was going to happen either to me or to a patient as a result of me missing something. And at that point, I broke down during rounds. I physically slowed my pace, dragged behind the team, and I broke down in tears because I felt like my dream was ending as I was not equipped to handle the volume or the pace. I wasn't smart enough, I wasn't fast enough, I wasn't good enough, and I wasn't strong enough. I didn't have the endurance that the other first-year medical residents did. I came to the realization that if not this, then what?

Fortunately, my resident saw my dismay. He took me to the chief resident, and within 20 minutes of her telling me how much confidence they had in me, and giving me a week off from the service and starting me back on with less patient volume, plus some counseling along the way, I was able to break through and live to fight another day.

I was able to get my feet solidly under me. In a week or two, I was able to go back to that medical service, push through, succeed and build confidence along the way. I was able to really resurrect my dream. That was a very dark time for me, not having much family support there and being confronted with the dreams slipping away. But I made it and thankfully, my greatest joy came that same year, some months later.

QUESTION: *What is one thing that you need to ask for help with? Let's make a deal that you'll ask for help today.*

RULE #4: PLAN THE WORK, THEN WORK THE PLAN!

Work hard to accomplish your own dreams. Nobody is going to give you anything. You need to work hard and earn it. When you do, you'll appreciate it that much more!

"If you can dream it, you can be it." I happen to think that's not true. In fact, I would say that you don't get what you dream, and I would even go as far as say, you probably don't deserve what you dream. What I mean by that is, you only get what you're willing to work for. So, it starts with a dream, true enough, but you must dream it, then you have to plan the work, and then you have to work the plan. Then, and only then, can you achieve it.

That's the part the quote often leaves out—implying that

you can dream it, and then you can be it, without all the hard work that comes in between. The truth is, there is a whole lot of hard work and sleepless nights.

QUESTION: *What is the most important goal you have right now? Do you have a written plan to accomplish it? If you need help, try using my (Dr. Dale's) G.R.I.N.D. strategy: Goals, Reason, Information, Network, Discipline.*

RULE #5: HAVE YOUR OWN VISION.

In life, you need to know what you want. If you don't know what you want, someone else will try to tell you what you want (i.e. what they want for you) and that might not be best for you!

Remember that the vision you have for yourself is the most important one. It's more important than the vision your parents have for you, more important than the vision that your partner or your spouse may have for you, more important than the vision your professor or your mentor has for you. It's your vision! It's the most important. People will often sell you short. They will often limit your potential because they're seeing it through their own sometimes limited potential or perspective.

QUESTION: *Whose vision are you trying to live out? Is it yours or someone else's?*

NOTES

_____

_____

_____

_____

_____

_____

_____

_____

_____

_____

_____

_____

_____

_____

_____

_____

_____

_____

_____

_____

DR. STEVEN SPENCER

Specialty:
Emergency Medicine

RULE #1: RECOGNIZE YOUR MAGICAL MOMENTS!

There are certain moments in life that simply wow you! Moments that give you a feeling like no other. A sense of awe and joy at the same time. These are the magical moments that can change your life. When they come, don't let them pass by. Take a moment to appreciate them.

When I was 9 years old, I had my first-ever allergic reaction to nuts. I was rushed to the hospital. One of the doctors saw me, talked to me a little bit, explained what he was going do, gave me some medication, and then I got better. To me, at that moment, I felt like it was magic. When you're a child and someone tells you, "I'm going to fix you!" and they fix you, it's magical. That's when I realized I wanted to be a doctor.

QUESTION: *What magical moment have you had within the past year? We all have them, and it's important we are aware and recognize them.*

RULE #2: WHEN TIMES GET TOUGH, FIND YOUR CHEERLEADERS.

In life, there will be trials and tribulations. At times, you'll be on the verge of quitting. You'll forget all about that magic moment that got you excited to pursue your dreams. When this happens, find your cheerleaders. To be successful, you need a network of people who have your best interest at heart and support you through thick and thin.

Medical school was tough for me. You spend so much time focusing on studying just medicine. I have so many other interests in life, so spending all my time on one thing was difficult. I took some time off from medical school. In fact, I thought about dropping out, but thanks to the encouragement from some of my classmates, some of my closest friends, and also Dean Williams, I didn't. She's passed now but she was an amazing woman at Meharry Medical School. She convinced me to keep pushing forward and let me know that there'd be a place in medicine for me.

But I still struggled. I always thought that I wasn't doing good . . . I wasn't doing good enough. She told me, "No, you're doing perfectly fine. You just got to keep up the work and keep pressing forward." So I did.

QUESTION: *Who is your number one cheerleader? Thank that person.*

RULE #3: HAVE EMOTIONS AND BE HUMAN.

We often try to trick ourselves into thinking we're superheroes. That doesn't do any good for anybody. Doctors are human also, and we have feelings. If you express emotions rather than keep them locked in, you'll be a better doctor.

The absolute hardest thing as an emergency physician to deal with is children dying. It's terrible. One time, I worked with a two-year-old who was in an accident and died, and I had to explain it to the parents. I watched the mother break down in tears. Those experiences stick with you, and those things make you cry. You're going to cry at work, you're going to come home and cry, and that's okay. That's just part of the job. That's you being human. But that's the hardest thing, overall.

QUESTION: *What makes you sad? What makes you happy? What makes you angry? What gives you the greatest feeling of love? Take all these things and use them to become great!*

RULE #4: ADVOCATE FOR THE VULNERABLE!

In our society, it is very easy for people to be overlooked, especially when they are viewed as having little to bring to the table. As a leader, it is your job to be the voice of the voiceless.

The absolute best thing about working as an emergency physician is when you definitively save a life. That's very rewarding. I remember once when I was a resident, there was a patient I wanted to admit to the hospital. She was a 55-year-old female patient with abdominal pain. I just I knew something was wrong, and the patient wasn't getting better. But no one, not the nurses, not my attending, no one wanted this patient to be admitted. They all thought she was full of it. But I had talked extensively to her and the family, and I knew something was off. So I dug my feet in the sand and forced the issue on everyone, including my attending. After some argument, I got the patient admitted to the medicine service. Within two hours of the admission, the patient started vomiting blood, crashed and wound up in the ICU. Had that happened at home, she would have died. The fact she was at the hospital when that happened made me very happy—that my hard work and persistence paid off.

QUESTION: *Who needs (or could benefit from) your help? What are you doing to help them?*

RULE #5: TREAT EVERYONE WITH RESPECT AND DO YOUR BEST FOR THEM.

We tend to treat people who don't like us poorly. Even worse, we treat people who we think don't like us poorly. But that's not what we're called to do. Everyone deserves to be treated with respect.

About one-fifth of my patients at the hospital center either have a Confederate flag on themselves, on one of their family members, or in the room somewhere I actually counted one time when I was a resident. But a lot of times those people were very nice and they let me treat them. And when they let me treat them, I treat them as best I possibly can. I try to go above and beyond the standard of care for just like I would anyone else. By doing that, I set an example as a positive and intelligent black character they see in their lives, hopefully that means something. I think, a lot of times, they may have different interpretations of history and a different worldview. But they're still people, they're still human beings, and they still deserve great care. That's what I try to do.

QUESTION: *Think of a time when someone gave you subpar service. How did it make you feel? Now think of a time when you gave someone else subpar service. How do you think it affected that person?*

NOTES

DR. DAVID KABITHE

Specialty:
General Surgery

RULE #1: FIND PEOPLE WHO BELIEVE IN YOU.

It's tough (but not impossible) to be successful when nobody believes in you. Sometimes, all it takes is finding that one person who does in order for you to blossom and shine!

I had to pass an entrance exam in English and math just to get into a public elementary school in Kenya. I passed the English test but failed the math test, so I was not accepted into the school that my younger siblings would go to. Mr. Fernandes, the principal, had the final say, and he said I wasn't qualified to attend that school based on my math test grade.

We visited several schools. The last school was much further away from home, called Langata West Primary School. I failed the math test there as well, but the principal of that school, Mrs. Wamwangi, decided to give me a chance. The teachers at that school were the first teachers to ever tell me that I was smart, and I listened. I was starting to see my potential and it was at this point that I thought, maybe I am smart.

QUESTION: *Who believes in you? Have you told them thank you?*

RULE #2: PRACTICE!

We've heard it a million times, practice makes perfect. But too often, we don't apply this to our intellect. Yes, it is possible to become smarter! All you need to do is practice!

I think people grow into their academic potential at different times and have different needs. If you are a young person who doesn't read well or you struggle with math, don't let that define you. With some help and more practice, you could become one of the best readers in your class or really good at math.

Like a basketball player must do different drills to be a good ball handler, with practice you can become a good reader and you can learn to develop good study skills. You could become a doctor, nurse, engineer, dentists, pharmacists, architect, accountant, lawyer—the list goes on and on. You can be more than you think you can be.

QUESTION: *What is one thing you spent a great deal of time practicing? Did you become good at that thing? What thing do you need to spend more time practicing now? Take the time today to figure out how you'll add more practice time for that into your schedule.*

RULE # 3: ASK FOR HELP.

This rule is pretty simple, yet many of us rarely do it. For some reason, we think we're weak if we need to ask for help. The truth is, the most successful people in the world are experts at asking for help.

Don't be ashamed or embarrassed to ask for help with reading or math like I was. Don't fit the description. Don't let anyone count you out, but most importantly, don't count yourself out.

QUESTION: *What do you need help with today? Ask for it!*

RULE #4: DON'T SETTLE.

Your future does not have to be your past.
The great thing about our lives is that we can
change them. Just because you used to be a
certain way doesn't mean you have to stay that way.
You always have the option to make yourself better.

I obtained my undergraduate education at Georgetown College, a small private liberal arts college in Kentucky, where I graduated with highest honors, summa cum laude. I went on to attend medical school at the University of Louisville School of Medicine, where I graduated with honors among the top students in my class.

If you met me in 1979 when I was in the sixth grade, you could never have imagined that I would achieve those accomplishments. You see, when I was in elementary school, I was not considered to be smart. I was not a good reader, I was very bad at math; and don't get me started on science, that was even worse.

QUESTION: *What is one thing you're settling for in life? Why are you settling instead of pursuing greatness?*

RULE #5: BELIEVE YOU CAN!

*There's a saying that goes: whether you
believe you can or believe you can't, you'll be right.
We all face challenges in life. When they come,
we have to believe we can take them on!*

At my school growing up, all the seventh graders took the test on the same day, at the same time. When the results came out, the schools were ranked, and it was announced on the news and in newspapers. My family and I were very worried about this exam. I received tutoring in math and had to learn new things like world geography and African history. With the teachers believing in me and their tutoring, I started to do well in school. I didn't do well in school in Kenya right away—it took time and hard work.

I was disciplined when necessary. The teachers believed in me, and I started to believe in myself. I realized my potential. It was around this time that I decided that I wanted to become a doctor because I now believed that I was smart. I really was smart! When it came time to take the national exam to get into high school, I was ready. The highest possible score was 36 points. I got 35 points.

QUESTION: *Do you believe you can be successful? Really believe?*

NOTES

DR. BYRON JASPER

Specialty:
Family Medicine

RULE #1: DON'T LET ANYONE TAKE WHAT YOU'VE EARNED.

There will come a time when you've done something great, and others will attribute credit elsewhere. While it's never good to have too much pride, you should not let others take advantage of you by denying you of what you've earned.

I was one of three valedictorians in my high school, but I didn't go to a high school that was majority-black. My high school, at best, was majority white and fairly even, in my opinion, when it came to opportunities. My mom set the tone early on to not give up my achievements.

Because I was the class president, in addition to being a valedictorian, I had speaking parts in multiple sections of the graduation ceremony. One of the administrators, approached me and said that even though I was the class president and had a lot of other achievements, I should give up one of my graduation speaking parts and let one of the other students do it so they could have a speaking opportunity as well, regardless of the fact that I earned the speaking parts. And me, being a high school student and not knowing any better, thought, well, it's not a big deal. I don't mind. But my mom told me: "No, you're going to go up there and you're going to say that part that you're supposed to say because you're the class president. You earned that opportunity. You don't let anyone take anything from you."

And from that moment, it stuck in my head that it wasn't something that was just as simple as giving somebody else an opportunity; it was more so giving up something I had earned.

QUESTION: *What have you worked hard for that someone else took the credit for? Would anything have been different if you had gotten the credit?*

RULE #2: SURROUND YOURSELF
WITH LIKE-MINDED PEOPLE.

Eagles fly with eagles, not with chickens. If you want to be successful, find your group of eagles to soar with!

When I got to Xavier University, a lot of people were smart like me, focused like me, motivated like me and planned to achieve their goals without just the hope that it could happen, but with the knowledge that it would happen. It's just a matter of time then it's going to happen.

Coming around people that look like you and talk like you and have similar experiences to you is very empowering. It gives you the idea that you're not alone, and sometimes that's very uplifting. It's also something that a lot of people don't realize can help others. A lot of students I teach and talk with nowadays often say: "Dr. Jasper, you don't realize just having you all come around and talk to us gives us a lot more motivation to keep going because we see somebody that looks like us and talks like us and comes from where we come from, and it gives us the mindset that we can do it."

I didn't realize how much that made sense until I got to Xavier. Being around my classmates and some of my friends gave me that mindset that if they are grinding, I need to grind, too.

QUESTION: *Name three friends who are like-minded to you. How much time do you spend with them compared with your other friends?*

RULE #3: BE READY TO TAKE ON YOUR DIFFICULTIES.

Many things worth having in life are difficult to achieve. Don't go into the battle thinking that it's going to be a cake walk. Always be ready to take on your challenges.

I got to med school, and it was a complete and utter wake-up call. I use the term "wake-up call" because I must have been sleeping the entire time I was there! Every time I tried and tried and tried to pass a class, I ran into a brick wall. You'd have to be asleep to keep hitting as many brick walls as I did—it was like a coin toss whether or not I was going to pass a class. It made no sense to me because, previous to med school, I had a 4.0 GPA in high school and was a valedictorian and 3.6 at Xavier University and graduated cum laude. So, I was in med school literally sitting there looking like a zombie half the time, trying to figure out what was wrong.

I studied countless hours—I literally lost count how many times I would study and not sleep. Other times, I stayed up late and woke up even earlier than most, continuing to study, only to get to the test and still have no idea what was going on. It was always a crapshoot. I felt defeated. It was mind-numbing to second-guess yourself. I wondered, "why am I here?" What am I doing? Should I keep pushing forward? Because I'm not really doing well like I used to.

That's a wake-up call for a lot of people when I tell them that part of the story. Many don't realize that I had such a hard time at one point. They may think that couldn't have happened because I'm one of the smartest people they know. "Yeah, that might be true," I tell them. "But we all have difficulties, and my difficulty was definitely medical school."

QUESTION: *What difficulty should you be preparing to tackle now?*

RULE #4: IT'S ABOUT THE JOURNEY, NOT THE FAILURES.

Unless your name is Jesus, you're going to fail at some point in life. The important thing is what you do after the failures. Remember, these are opportunities for growth.

And all of those things that came along with the failures basically melted away. I was able to say: "Look, I made it, you can make it, too."

At the end of the day, it's not about the failures; it's about the journey. I told that part of my story to give people the understanding that you can do anything you put your mind to! You can get through any obstacle in front of you, but you have to keep going. I could have quit the first time, the second time or the third time. I could have quit before the fourth time. But if you are meant to do this, and you really want to do this, you can! But it's never going to be easy.

QUESTION: *What has been your biggest "failure" in the past year? What did you learn from it?*

RULE #5: DON'T GIVE UP.

The only way to guarantee failure is to not try or to give up. When you face challenging times on your journey to success, envision what things will be like once you've achieved your goal. Don't give up!

If that isn't ironic, I don't know what it is. The same person who had trouble learning how to take a standardized test is the same person teaching people how to pass standardized tests! I'm the person mentoring other students on how not to make the mistakes that I did. I'm also trying to help others understand that this Medicine is an art form and not just something you can get from a standardized exam. If you've made it this far, don't give up. If you are reading this and you made it to med school but are struggling, know that I was you. I was the person thinking they could do anything and then got knocked for a loop.

QUESTION: *What are you thinking about giving up on? Why do you want to give up? Is that a valid reason? What might your life look like if you don't give up?*

NOTES

EMMANUEL MCNEELY

Medical Student

RULE # 1: ACADEMICS BEFORE EXTRACURRICULARS!

*In today's society, so many of us get caught up in
extracurriculars. That often means sports, sports and more
sports. But the reality is, most of us won't play professional
sports. And even if you do, that only lasts for a few years,
then your sports career is done. That's why academics should
be more important than sports in your life.*

During my high school years, I played sports, but they were secondary. My number one was academics, academics, academics. Rather than participate in varsity football, I worked at a local hospital. I even won a scholarship to continue working at the cancer hospital, where I worked as a pharmacy technician for a total of three years.

At that point, I was interested in pharmacy, but I sought out one of the physicians there who allowed me to go into his surgery. He showed me a routine cholecystectomy procedure (which is removing gallstones from a gallbladder). I was 18 years old, and I switched my focus: I want to be a surgeon. Little did I know what that entailed. I didn't know any African American physicians.

QUESTION: *What extracurricular activity is getting in the way of your educational/developmental progress?*

RULE #2: CHASE YOUR DREAMS.

*Literally, go after them! Sometimes you have to go
through amazing obstacles to reach your dream.
Don't let anything get in your way!*

I needed to transfer to another school. I reapplied to my "dream school" but did not get accepted. I applied to another school in South Florida and got accepted. They had a research chemistry degree, and I love chemistry.

So, in 2009, my dad and I drove from Chicago, Illinois, to South Florida where I got a second shot in pursuing my dream of becoming a surgeon.

QUESTION: *What dream are you chasing? Now be honest— how hard are you running after it?*

RULE # 3: FOCUS!

We all want to be superhuman. By that I mean, we want to do everything and be the best at everything. Jack of all trades, master of none. To become great at something, you need to focus.

I took 18 credit hours and worked 20 hours a week in a pharmacy that was about 45 minutes away. I was still very involved in my church and I was very busy with school. What happens when you have a lot on your plate, you're 18 years old, and you're not focusing on one thing? I was just an average student. I probably had a low B average GPA. For everyone listening out there, you need to do the absolute best you can with your coursework if you want to pursue medicine. This isn't something everyone says because it sounds good. You will be evaluated from day one until the last day before you apply to go to the next position, the next level, and the next school. Do not close doors on yourself because you didn't fully apply yourself. That's an important lesson I had to learn. In essence, I lacked focus due to poor time management.

QUESTION: *What is your biggest distraction? What can you do to minimize it?*

RULE #4: DON'T TAKE NO FOR AN ANSWER.

Throughout your life, you'll likely be told "no" more times than you're told "yes." It tends to be the default answer for many people. But here's a little secret—you don't have to accept that!

I applied everywhere for a job. Stayed at a friend's house and slept on his couch. All my stuff was in garbage bags and it was a hundred degrees outside. Every time I had a job interview, I would head to the basement and rifle through all the garbage bags until I found a tie, a dress sock, the matching dress sock, plus iron the suit over and over again.

Remember the movie, *The Pursuit of Happyness,* where the Will Smith character kept getting rejected? That's how I felt. Everyone said, "No. No. No, you're a chemistry major. What are you going to do in this field? No. No. No."

Again, I couldn't get a job with my former school. So I networked and found a car dealership where I thought I could at least make money to live on. Long story short, after five interviews, persistently going back to them, calling them every single day at the exact same time, they took a guy with a chemistry degree to sell vehicles. I trained there, and worked there in what turned out to be a very hard season in my life. Some weeks I would work 70 hours;

I learned how to deal with difficult people. That's one thing I took from that job. But that being said, I did well.

QUESTION: *What have you accepted a "no" answer to in the past year which you regret? What do you think would have happened if you did not take "no" for an answer?*

RULE #5: DO NOT STOP! DO NOT QUIT!

To be a person of consistent success, you must have resolve. Having resolve means that once you've decided to do something, you won't stop until it's done. Life has many challenges and having the resolve to take them on is essential for success.

A five-year winding road that seemed so long while I was in the middle of it. I didn't know how long it was going to take me to finally get where I wanted to be. Now, I am in a position to start my dream of becoming a medical doctor and a surgeon.

So, for anyone out there, my message to you is: Do not stop, do not quit. I could have stopped at 17 when that teacher brought me to the back of the class when I was impressionable and had a pure heart and just wanted to do my best. I could have stopped when those advisors looked at me in the face and laughed at me.

I could have stopped when my dream undergrad school denied me, three times total. I could have stopped at any point when I ran out of money, or when people laughed when I couldn't get a job at my undergrad school. I could have done any of that. I could have stopped at any point if people would have said, "Yeah, Emmanuel, you're smart, you tried. Okay, do something else." But I wanted to be a physician. A made-up mind is a strong thing. Do not let anyone dictate your future but YOU. Do not let anyone tell you that you can't do something. Pray, work hard and find mentors.

When I didn't do well on my MCAT, I literally Googled black doctors on YouTube, and for hours and hours what came up? Diverse Medicine came up. Dr. Dale came up! Black Men in White Coats came up. After every video I said to myself: "There's someone who did what I'm trying to do. I can be that person."

QUESTION: *What are you on the verge of stopping because you are scared to fail or simply tired of pursuing? What do you need to do in order to keep on fighting? How can you get the energy to keep on pushing?*

NOTES

_____

_____

_____

_____

_____

_____

_____

_____

_____

_____

_____

_____

_____

_____

_____

_____

_____

_____

_____

_____

_____

_____

DR. JASON ROBINSON

Specialty:
Hospital Medicine

RULE #1: DON'T EXPECT EVERYONE TO SUPPORT YOU.

Not everybody will be happy about your success. People will turn against you because they are jealous. On your road to greatness, do not expect everyone to support you. There will be haters, and you can't let them slow you down.

After my first year in college, I applied to the early assurance program, which allowed me to enter medical school without taking the MCAT. Anyone who's attempted to go to med school or has gone to medical school knows that the MCAT is an extremely difficult test, and a lot of times people stop there.

Entering my second year of undergrad, I had already been accepted to medical school. I never told many people that I'd been accepted—only my very close friends. A very good friend of mine was extremely proud when she found out, and she began telling people. Then I was treated very badly by some people. After that, you would expect people to cheer for me, but a lot of my white classmates couldn't believe it and made it a point to tell me that they couldn't believe that I was smart enough to achieve something like that.

I spent the last three years of college pretty much being on my own. Being by myself. I never got much moral support or help from my classmates.

QUESTION: *Who in your life isn't supporting you? Who can you have real conversations with to discuss your feelings?*

RULE #2: STAY HUMBLE.

Stay humble or else you'll be humbled. At some point prior to medical school, many now doctors were considered smarter than their classmates. This makes it easy for them to want to brag. The thing about medical school however, is once you're there, you realize that everyone else around you is just as smart! Even if you earn better grades than everyone else, remember to stay humble!

I was still an academic stud. Everything that I did, I did well. It wasn't uncommon for people to say, "He's the smartest black kid on campus" or "He's one of the smartest black kids at school."

In 1998, I entered medical school and my first test was gross anatomy. It was very humbling. I realized that I wasn't that much of an academic stud after all, plus there were nothing but academic studs around me. It was a great equalizer. I realized I wasn't all that, and I was going to have to work really, really, really hard—harder than I ever did before.

QUESTION: *Think of time in the past week when you were not humble. Why did you behave the way that you did? What is one thing you can always do to remind yourself to stay humble?*

RULE #3: DON'T TORTURE YOURSELF.

It's important to know when enough is enough. There will be difficult times in life when you must push through rough

*situations. You'll butt heads with people and simply
have to deal with it. However, there are other times when
people mistreat you to the point that you begin to feel
miserable and it becomes bad for your health. In those
situations, it's okay to move on to the next opportunity
rather than torture yourself.*

I returned to Dallas and signed probably the worst hospitalist contract a doctor could sign. I was working 28 days a month. Routinely, I was on call every other night. Probably every other call, I had to get out of my bed and go to a hospital because somebody was critically sick or someone was admitted to the ICU. It was a really, really rough time; it was a hard time. I couldn't sleep in the room with my wife because my beeper went off so often.

To be honest, I was only tolerating one of the hospitals where I worked. All the doctors were mean. For example, I'd call for a consult and they'd ask, "Why do I need to see this patient?" Uh, because I asked you to see this patient? Most of my patients were uninsured or underinsured, so the doctors knew they weren't going to get paid . . . they were just mean.

I finally had enough. I thought, *I'm out of here.* I was working every day, I was up every other night. It was ridiculous. I put in my notice to my group, and they were very disappointed. They tried to do what they could to get me to stay, but I couldn't. I needed to find another job. I couldn't tolerate working in that hospital anymore.

QUESTION: *What unnecessary stress are you putting yourself through? How do you plan to get out of that stressful situation?*

RULE #4: BE PROUD OF YOUR ACCOMPLISHMENTS:

On your journey to success, you'll accomplish many great things. It is human nature for us to want others to acknowledge what we've done, but the reality is that most great things we do will go unnoticed. Be proud of your own accomplishments; you don't need validation from others.

Be proud of your accomplishments. I don't care how small or how big, be proud of them because you did it. And when you get stuck—because you're going to get stuck—you're going to be afraid you're going to fail, you're going to have doubt, and you're going to look at yourself as a loser. Having all those feelings and those thoughts and being in those situations are okay. They're a stepping stone because they give you an opportunity to conquer something, whether it's a fear or a failure. But when you come out on the other side, you'll be stronger.

QUESTION: *What has been your biggest accomplishment in the past week? Write yourself a short note of congratulations.*

RULE #5: KEEP MOVING.

Let's be real—we're all going to fail at a lot of things in life. During these times, it's easy to want to quit and simply stop trying. Don't do that! Take it one step at a time, and you can get to your goal. Just keep moving, even if you have to crawl.

When you get to those times when you're stuck, and you've reached out to everybody you can, and you feel like you've done everything to conquer this, sometimes you have to accept that you have to simply move past it. The thing you don't want to do is stand still, so just keep moving. Take one step. That's the way I've lived my life.

I like to think to myself that nobody fails more than I do. I fail at being a physician, I fail at being a husband, I fail at being a father, I fail at being a brother. But the thing I don't fail at is trying. I keep taking one step. Keep putting one foot in front of the other, and that will take you to places that you can never imagine.

QUESTION: *What area of life do you feel stuck in? What needs to be done to get the ball rolling again?*

NOTES

_____

_____

_____

_____

_____

_____

_____

_____

_____

_____

_____

_____

_____

_____

_____

_____

_____

_____

_____

_____

_____

_____

DR. STEPHEN NOBLE

Specialty:
Cardiothoracic Surgery

RULE #1: BE CURIOUS!

Good doctors are curious people. The ability to ask "why" separates good clinicians from average ones. This curiosity typically begins at an early age and stays with the individual throughout their career.

When I was 5 years old, I remember at my grandparents' house they had an encyclopedia that I would flip through every time I visited. In one particular section was the human body, including transparency pages you could flip around to see the different systems. I would look at it for hours, flipping from the skeletal system, then the nervous system, then the cardiovascular system and the lymphatic system. I would look at that thing over and over again.

It really sparked an interest in me. I wanted to know, why did things work? Why was the human body the way that it was? Why do people get sick? Why do people die? Why do people get illnesses? Why did they need surgery? I always had a fascination with the human body. That always stuck with me.

And so, one of my earliest memories of wanting to go into medicine was trying to figure out the answers as to why things happened.

QUESTION: *What are you most curious about? How do you think this will help you in your future profession?*

RULE #2: READ, READ, READ!

One of the easiest ways to gain exposure to something is by reading. Sure, it's not the same as actually living it, however, a vicarious experience is better than no experience.

I eventually went on to read the book *Gifted Hands* by Dr. Ben Carson when I was in junior high school. Reading that book reaffirmed that I want to be a doctor. I didn't know what kind of doctor I wanted to be, I just knew that I wanted to be a doctor. And by reading the book, it showed me that I could do it.

I don't have any physicians in my family. My grandmother was a nurse at Oregon Health Science University, working in the operating rooms as well as on the cardiac surgery floors. My other grandmother worked in a cafeteria at the hospital. So I don't have any physician mentors or family members who are doctors. But reading the book, Gifted Hands, showed me that with faith, due diligence and putting in hard work, I could make it.

QUESTION: *What is one book that you have been wanting to read? Can you start reading it now?*

RULE #3: PLAN AHEAD.

The proverb says, "where there is no vision, the people perish." The basic idea here is that you must look to the future and know what you want. Once you've decided what you want, plan how you're going to get it.

I had an American history teacher who really imparted to me the importance of planning and setting out a five and 10-year plan. In high school, I set out the plan of what it would take for me to be a physician. I knew going to college was definitely something that I had to do if I was going to go to medical school.

And so, my 10-year plan in high school had me being in medical school 10 years from then. Four years of college and another four years of medical school. And it came true! I had the plan of being a physician and doing residency. Planning and preparation was key.

QUESTION: *Where do you see yourself in five years? 10 years?*

RULE #4: PROVE THEM WRONG.

Other people think they know what you are capable of, but they're often way off. You're much more capable of accomplishing tasks than even you know. When someone tells you that you can't do something, prove them wrong.

When it came time for my general surgery rotation, I fell in love with it. And this was something that I was really leaning towards. I recall scrubbing in one time and getting ready to do a transplant surgery with one of the transplant fellows. Basically, he was one of those individuals who had finished general surgery residency and was doing his specialty training in transplant surgery. We were at the scrub sink, washing our hands and the fellow asked, "What are you going to go into?"

I told him, "I'm leaning towards surgery."

His response was, "You're not going to go into surgery. You either know it or you don't. Someone just doesn't lean towards going into surgery and succeed."

By him doubting me, it brought up all those memories back in junior high school of my teachers thinking I couldn't do advanced math. And it was really at that scrub sink that I thought to myself, *you know what, I'm going to do surgery.* This person doubted me. I do like surgery, I do enjoy it, so I'm going to do it. Right then and there, at the scrub sink, getting ready to do a transplant case, I made the decision, I was going into surgery.

QUESTION: *Has anyone ever doubted you? How did that make you feel? Are you ready to prove them wrong?*

RULE #5: BE A TOOL FOR GOD.

I truly appreciated Dr. Noble's view on this.
It's easy to go through life without spending time
thinking about why you are here. There is a higher
power who has an agenda. Our job is to do what we're
called to do and be a tool for God's work.

My greatest joy has been my patients. After you finish an operation and you see patients doing well, that by far is the greatest joy. It's really the culmination of all the hard work and it feels as if you are a tool of God. I feel so fortunate to do what I do because I feel it's a calling that God has put me on this path. Healing someone is spiritual and it's emotional. The hard work that goes into it and seeing patients do well is great. It truly does make it all worth it.

For those of you out there on the road, my biggest pieces of advice are: first, have faith in a higher power, but also faith in yourself is important. Because there are going to be moments in which you doubt yourself, in which people doubt you, but having faith in who you are and in your dreams is important. Mentorship is key. It's important to have mentors! I've had a mentor every step along the way. I have mentors even to this day that I go to for advice."

QUESTION: *In what way is God using you?*

NOTES

DR. ANDRE CAMPBELL

Specialty:
Trauma Surgery

RULE #1: FIND SOMEONE WHO WILL PUSH YOU TO DO YOUR BEST.

It's easy for us to say we're doing our best but never really push ourselves. However, if you can find someone who truly wants you to succeed, that person can push you to higher levels than you thought were possible.

I had some challenges in school, but as I entered the fourth grade, I ended up with an African-American teacher named Ms. Walker.

She challenged me to be successful. She would never take less than your best effort. She would always say, "You can do better, you can do better." The fact that she knew that I could do better really propelled me towards what I needed to be successful.

So, coming out of fourth grade, I was then able to place at the higher end of the classes at the school I was at in Queens.

QUESTION: *Who is the person in your life that will push you to perform at your highest level?*

RULE #2: DON'T RUSH.

It is difficult to achieve greatness. You'll face challenges along the way and sometimes you just need to take a break and slow down. Don't rush success.

I had a lot of challenges in school. My father was ill. I had a number of things that were going on. I had to work throughout my whole college experience. I worked about 10 to 15 hours a week on top of all the science classes. But as I went through my third and fourth year, some issues came up, I decided I would take an extra year off between college and medical school.

During that time, I worked as a counselor. I also lined up a job doing research.

QUESTION: *What is one area of your life that you feel rushed in? What can you do to slow down and still be successful in that area?*

RULE #3: GO AFTER WHAT YOU WANT.

We don't always know what we want in life. Sometimes we think we do, but then it changes. When that happens, it's perfectly fine to change your plans and go after what you really want! Dr. Campbell initially thought he wanted to be an internal medicine doctor, which is different from becoming a surgeon. In order to become either one of these types of doctors, you must apply to what is often called the "Match." The match for internal medicine is completely different than it is for surgery. The way the match works is that you apply to training programs, interview at some, then list the ones you like in a "rank" list and the computer matches you with a program.

I entered my third year and I still had this burning desire to be a surgeon. And with the help of John and my professors at the University of California San Francisco,

I ended up going back to the Match. This time I applied to 10 programs.

I interviewed at a bunch, but some of the experiences were not great. In fact, some people thought that they wouldn't take a chance on me, and a lot of places said no. Thinking through things, I decided that I was going to rank only three places, which I now realize was totally wrong. In fact, I was embarrassed after I did it.

Looking back on it now, what that means is that there's a chance that I wouldn't be talking to you now as a surgeon. I took a chance like that, and it was the wrong thing for me to do. Right now, I tell my students apply to 25 places, and go to 10 to 15 interviews.

I told one of my mentors at Columbia, Dr. Ford, what I did. "You did what?" He was flabbergasted.

When I went to the Match again, I applied, and it turned out that I matched with Colombia for surgery!

QUESTION: *What is one thing that you want in life but have been too scared to go after? Are you in a position to go for it now?*

RULE #4: GET UP.

We're all going to get knocked down in life.
The key to success is getting back up!

No matter what you choose to do, you must be excellent, and you always have to be excellent. Be excellent in what you do. Be the best you can be. Every day, your patients will challenge you and you will try to be the best. All they want you to give is a hundred percent all the time.

Throughout my whole career, I've had a lot of challenges. From where I ended up in residency, going through two residencies, getting into medical school, high school, college—challenges on so many different steps of the way. I have just one message I want to leave with you. It isn't that you have to win all the time, but if you get knocked over, it's about how you get up and how many times you get up. You must get up afterwards. You must shake yourself off and go forward.

QUESTION: *Think of one example in the past month when you got knocked down. Did you get back up? If not, can you get up now?*

RULE #5: BE EXCITED ABOUT WHAT YOU DO.

People perform better when they're excited about what they do. Figure out what excites you and do that!

Every day at the hospital, I get to do great things. I get to save lives and make people better. I get a chance to stamp out disease and make the world a better place. I've always had the feeling that the reason why I went into surgery is because I wanted to ride in on my white horse and save the day. And I've been able to do that during my career. I basically identify problems, take care of patients, and make them better. I get a chance to do it every day, and it is an honor to be a physician. It's really an outstanding career and I have a wonderful time doing what I do.

QUESTION: *What gets you most excited? How are you incorporating that into your day to day life to benefit others?*

NOTES

DR. CEDREK MCFADDEN

Specialty:
Colorectal Surgery

RULE #1: DREAM!

Reality starts with an idea. Don't limit your imagination. Don't hold it back. Dream away!

Certainly, as you dream about being a doctor, you have a sense that you want to help and make things better. As a child, seeing my grandmother go through an illness, I often wanted to find ways to be helpful. Putting all of that together created something in me; by the time I was in late junior high, I recognized that I wanted to be a doctor. I don't think I thought about the challenges. I just thought *I want to be a doctor* and so I began to say that, and I began to believe that. And even in high school, I remember taking certain tests where they asked, "What you want to be?" And I remember clicking "doctor." But it wasn't that I had this thought out plan set in place. It was simply a thought, and as I began to think it, I said it; and as I said it, I believed it and really set the course for what I wanted to do.

QUESTION: *What dreams do you have which you're too embarrassed to share with others? In your perfect world, what would you want to do? Why not go for it?*

RULE #2: BE PROACTIVE.

Life is full of great opportunities. Don' wait for them to come to you. Instead, be proactive and go get them.

A teacher of mine saw a CNN report about Xavier University in Louisiana and, how they were number one for admissions of black students into medical school. She told me about it with so much enthusiasm, it impressed on me that I should really check the school out. So that's what I did. This was before internet, so I called the school. They sent a handbook with very little information, but I became impressed at this program at Xavier University. It seemed to be a good fit for what I needed. The excitement that I had about medicine about being a doctor, they really poured into that. Once I applied and got accepted, that's where I chose to go.

QUESTION: *What opportunity have you been letting slip past you? How can you be proactive to take advantage of it?*

RULE #3: DO THE THINGS THAT ARE IMPORTANT TO YOU.

One of the biggest regrets doctors often have is letting go of their passions or not spending time on the things that are important to them. Just because you're working hard to accomplish a goal doesn't mean you can't keep your passions. Don't let go of what's important to you!

I was blessed to be involved with ministry in New Orleans. I had always been involved in ministry, in church with my family. It was important to me that I continued that in college because it really created a sense of foundation that I needed. It provided a sense of encouragement and support that I don't think I would have done well without. The ministry helped me stay focused and attentive to what I needed to do. Knowing that I had a church service to go to at a certain time, I used the time wisely. That was my college life.

QUESTION: *What is the most important thing that you want to do in life? Can you do it while pursuing other dreams?*

RULE #4: GET INSPIRED!

People lack motivation because they don't look for things that inspire them. For every goal, there is something out there that can inspire you to achieve it. Figure out what inspires you and use that as your fuel to drive you to success.

Everyone who got accepted to medical school were featured in a class case in a lobby of the science center. So, from the time I was a freshman, day in and day out, I walked into the science building and saw these pictures and where they were going to medical school. It would say "John Smith has been accepted to Howard University School of Medicine," or whatever it may be. I saw that throughout the year. So, by the time I became a junior, it was ingrained in me that I wanted my face and name to be in this glass case! The expectation had been set from freshman year. I think that was a fantastic thing.

QUESTION: *What inspires you the most? What one thing can you do to make sure that inspiration stays close to you?*

RULE #5: BE RESPONSIBLE FOR YOUR OWN JOURNEY.

Whether or not you're successful is on you! Nobody's coming to give a participation trophy. It's your job to succeed!

I've learned through this journey that you have to sometimes say something before you can believe it and see it. And, you have to continue the journey that you believe is best for you, despite what other folks may tell you. Even if other folks doubt your abilities, believe and move forward and prove people wrong. I'm not saying that necessarily has to be your goal, but I think that has to be your mantra, that you are responsible for your journey.

QUESTION: *What excuses have you been making about why you're not as successful as you'd like to be? We all have some.*

NOTES

DR. ADELEKE ADESINA

Specialty:
Emergency Medicine

RULE #1: **DO WHAT YOU CAME TO DO.**

Step 1 in achieving anything is knowing what that thing is.
Set your mind on the goal, and don't stop until you get it.
Do what you came to do!

I moved from Nigeria to the United States looking for a better life and to pursue my career path of becoming a doctor. I started in a small private school called Bloomfield College. My freshman year, I walked into my advisor's office and said, "Ma'am, I came from Nigeria and I want to be a doctor." She laughed at me.

She said, "What do you mean you want to be a doctor? Do you know what it takes to become a doctor? Have you ever taken the MCAT? Do you know what the Health Care system in America is like?"

I said, "Ma'am, I have no idea but all I know is I want to become a physician."

She said, "Becoming a doctor is one of the most difficult things people ever do in this country. Plus, you don't have a green card."

I said, "Well, that's beside the point. I came to this country because I want to become a doctor and that's the reason why I'm here."

She was shocked. People are going to tell you no. A lot of people are going to turn you down; they are not going to believe in your dreams. You have to believe in yourself.

QUESTION: *What did you come to do? Are you doing it?*

RULE #2: TAKE CHARGE OF YOUR OWN LIFE.

We live in a world where we're made to believe that other people know more about what we're doing than we do. We are constantly seeking advice and letting others make decisions for us. The advice part is good but letting them make your decisions is bad. Take charge of your own life.

I said, "Ma'am, listen, give me a chance. I want to start at the chemistry two level and if I even get a C, pull me out of the course." She said, "Absolutely not."

"I got a 3.5 GPA last semester."

She said, "Well that doesn't mean anything. You took math, English, and biology. I'm not impressed."

That was my second obstacle. So, I said, "Well, I don't want to spend five years in college. I want to spend four years in college and graduate on time so I can get to medical school."

At the end of the semester, I got a 3.9 GPA. I went back to my advisor's office and said, "Listen, look at my GPA. I've taken anatomy and physiology, and I've taken calculus one."

And she said, "Oh, well, I'm impressed. Maybe I should have allowed you to take that chemistry course, but guess what? You're going to start with chemistry one."

I said, "Okay, but guess what? I'm going to be changing the rules from now on. I'm going to take charge of my life. I'm going to start to make my own schedule."

QUESTION: *Who is making the decisions in your life? Are you in charge?*

RULE #3: MAKE SOMEONE PROUD.

None of us become successful on our own. Always remember the people who helped you and aim to make them proud.

When my pre-med advisor heard that I got into medical school, she was very happy for me. Although she couldn't believe it, she was very happy. She helped me with my application process. She wrote me letters of recommendation. She doubted me for a very long time, but eventually, I finally broke through and she accepted me. She said, "You did it. I'm proud of you."

Those words meant a lot to me. I went on to medical school to do extremely well.

QUESTION: *Who do you want to make proud? Why?*

RULE #4: COUNT THE COST.

Anything worthwhile will take a great deal of work. Before you decide to go all in, count the cost. Make sure you're prepared for the challenges ahead!

When you make that decision that you want to become a doctor, remember that you're signing up for a big task. As soon as you say that, people around you are going to ask, "Do you know how long it takes to become a doctor? It takes about 11 to 17 years. That is a long time." Well, that is their time perspective. I didn't see it that way. I saw my dreams. I knew if I work hard enough, long enough and somebody gave me a chance and an opportunity and I didn't give up, I was going to make it. Most people in life go through the path of least resistance. They want to do something that's easy.

Well, becoming a physician is not easy. It is hard. It is difficult. But you know what? Nobody told you it was going be easy. If you're going to have people's lives in your hands, it's not going to come easy. You're going to sacrifice hours and hours of your time reading nonstop, giving and sweating. But in the end, it's really sweet. The compensations are absolutely wonderful. You're going to live a great life.

QUESTION: *What will it cost you to achieve your dream? Is it worth it?*

RULE# 5: LEARN FROM YOUR MISTAKES.

The great thing about life is that we get a lot of do-overs. When something doesn't go your way, take the time to figure out why so you can do better the next time around.

Learn from your mistakes. You're going to make a lot of mistakes and things are not going to come easy to you. But in the end, everything will work out. Don't give up, don't give in, even if you fail the MCAT once, twice, three times. Don't give up. But remember, don't keep making the same mistakes. If you fail twice, find out exactly, what you are doing wrong, and keep working hard at it. Experts are called experts because they are spending thousands of hours trying to master the same subject over and over.

QUESTION: *What is one mistake you have made in the past year that you have learned from?*

NOTES

_____

_____

_____

_____

_____

_____

_____

_____

_____

_____

_____

_____

_____

_____

_____

_____

_____

_____

_____

_____

_____

_____

_____

DR. NII DARKO

Specialty:
Trauma Surgery

RULE #1: TAKE YOUR EDUCATION SERIOUSLY.

Education is the key to opportunity. Many people have achieved great things in life simply because they took their education seriously. And by education, I don't mean just school. You should always be learning, in and out of the classroom. It opens doors to success!

My mother and my father are both blue-collar immigrants from Ghana, West Africa. My mother is a nursing assistant. My father is a computer technician. From a very early age, education was pressed hard on me, as well as my three older sisters. In order for us to make it out of the projects and in the city, my parents said the best way to do this was to really educate yourself and take yourself from one station in life to another more successful, comfortable portion of your life. That really resonated with me.

QUESTION: *Are you serious about your education? What is one thing you can start doing today that demonstrates this?*

RULE #2: IF YOU CAN SEE IT, YOU CAN BE IT.

The saying goes, you can't be what you can't see. Looking at that from another angle, if you can see it, you can be it. That's true even if you only see it on television.

When I was growing up, I wanted to be so many different things. Being an athlete was something that I was considering, then at one point, I wanted to be an actor, and even one point, I wanted to be an astronaut. But to be honest the one thing that really stood out to me was the concept, the idea, of Dr. Heathcliff Huxtable from *The Cosby Show*, a very popular TV show in the 1980s.

As a family, we would sit in front of the TV and watch. I didn't personally know any black doctors when I was growing up. So to see a black man on TV who was a doctor, with a beautiful wife who was a lawyer, plus they had kids, that were cool and they all lived in a brownstone in Brooklyn; I was hooked. I knew that's the type of life that I wanted, and I couldn't specifically pinpoint exactly what aspect I liked the most, but this was a life that I wanted for myself. And I'm going to be very honest—I didn't know anything about being a doctor aside from what I saw on TV.

QUESTION: *Close your eyes. Can you see your success? Really, can you??? Do this exercise three times today.*

RULE #3: GET REAL LIFE EXPERIENCE.

No matter how much you read about something or see it on television, there's nothing like the real deal. Find a way to get in the game and get real life experience.

I got a chance to meet an alumni named was Dr. Jordan Garrison, a trauma surgeon at University Hospital in Newark, New Jersey. He was a physician practicing literally five blocks away from my house. I asked if I could shadow him for a little bit. I finally got a chance to watch him. He invited me to come down and spend an evening there. I still remember my parents dropping me off at the hospital.

I remember talking to Dr. Garrison, probably for about

three to five minutes, then his pager started going off and some alarm went off in the hallway, and we quickly went down to the ED. By the time we got there, he put a gown on me. "Hey, stay in that corner right there and just watch what I do, but don't move. You'll be okay."

QUESTION: *What is your plan to get real-life experience? If you already have experience, what is your plan to get more of it?*

RULE #4: FIGHT THROUGH THE SHAME.

When things don't go your way, it can be very embarrassing and shameful. Find a way to keep your confidence and fight your way through that shame.

I experienced some tough times in college. I had to apply to medical school twice. And there was self-doubt and shame that grew from that. Before I got rejected the first time, I told everybody that I wanted to be a physician, I wanted to be a surgeon. But when I got rejected, I didn't want to share that story with anybody anymore.

Anytime someone brought up my dreams of what I wanted to do, I would change the subject. But I finally picked myself up. I applied the second time. I changed my strategy and I got in.

QUESTION: *We all have shame. How has your shame held you back? How do you plan on moving forward without the shame?*

RULE #5: ALWAYS REMEMBER
IT'S ABOUT HELPING PEOPLE.

A lot of things drive us to be successful. Money, power, and respect are among the most common. But in the end, above all of those things should be our desire to serve and help people.

Some of the best times were related to what I did in the operating room and what I did even before the operating room. But the times that I really remember were afterward. For example, getting a hug from a patient's family member because I spent an additional two hours explaining everything from what happened in the operating room to what to expect afterward. This was two hours past my shift, but I didn't care. Being able to get a hug for helping them to understand that we've got some tough times ahead but we're going to be okay, I'm not going to leave them by themselves—those moments were really rewarding and there's truly nothing like it.

QUESTION: *Who can you help today? How will you help this person?*

NOTES

DR. BRIAN J. DIXON

Specialty:
Psychiatry

RULE #1: STRIVE TO DO BETTER
THAN WHERE YOU CAME FROM!

This should be true regardless your upbringing. The goal should always be to do better. Make no excuses about what you had or didn't have. Just do better!

We grew up on food stamps and the whole nine yards. I think we were one step above welfare at any given moment because my mom was very proud of what she was able to accomplish and keep us out of. I thought that was wonderful. But it did mean that there were lots of hard days. Growing up, we never really went to the doctor. That's partly because we couldn't afford it, but also partly because my mom was able to find ways to keep us from having to go to the doctor. One of the books that stood out to me from my childhood was called *The Doctor's Book of Home Remedies*. In it were lots of different ideas of how to help with illness. Since I had lots of allergy issues and sinus infections, I remember reading that book cover to cover learning about all sorts of things. I thought that was a really nice way of empowering people, even though at the time I didn't call it that because I didn't know that term. But after living through summers in east Texas with no air conditioning and no running water and seeing people who were addicted to drugs . . . once you live through all that, you know you got to do something different for your life, something better.

QUESTION: *Are you on pace to be better than where you came from? If not, what can you do to get on the right track?*

RULE #2: FIND A QUOTE THAT INSPIRES YOU.

Words are powerful! A simple sentence can spark genius. A simple sentence can motivate someone to achieve greatness. Identify a quote that pushes you to excellence.

Henry David Thoreau said, "The best thing a man can do for his culture when he is rich, is to endeavor to carry out those schemes which he entertained when he was poor." That quote has inspired me for many years.

Growing up, I didn't realize how poor we were until I met my college friend, who took me to his lake house. His lake house was bigger than my actual house! You never really know where you fit in the social scheme of things until you run across other people. But I didn't let that stop me.

QUESTION: *What is your favorite motivational quote?*

RULE #3: GET ORGANIZED!

Jumping into a situation without being organized is a setup for disaster. Success takes calculated planning. It doesn't just happen on its own. Strategize, then organize.

If could speak to every single African American man that wanted to go to medical school, my advice would be to number one, believe in yourself. But mostly, as strange as it sounds, organize. We live in an age where the answers are out there; we have access to all the information in the world through our smartphones, through the internet. It's all there. The key is to organize that data. You need to get organized. It's great to go out and march. I think it's great to do your civic duty and vote. But if you want to succeed in medicine, if you want to succeed with any major lifelong project, you have to get organized.

I ran across this quote by Thomas Edison, "Vision without a plan is a hallucination." And that is so true. We can dream and hope as much as we want, but if we don't create a plan to execute, then it's all for naught. Get organized and keep in mind that there's going to be a lot of stuff that stands between you and your dreams.

QUESTION: *What area of your life is least organized? What can you do to fix that?*

RULE #4: DON'T BE SCARED TO GO AGAINST THE GRAIN AND DO THINGS THE WAY YOU BELIEVE IS BEST.

We work in systems and organizations that are not perfect. It's easy to get indoctrinated and think that the way our systems operate is the only right way and all others are wrong. That's often not true. Usually there's a better way to do something. Find that better way and do it!

I was raised to believe you get up every morning and go to work, and work was always owned by somebody—most times, by those who didn't look like you or who didn't think like you. Running my own business was such a foreign concept, and it seemed really terrifying. That little voice said, "You have to leave, you have to quit." I thanked the administrator for his comments, because you never burn bridges and I left.

I resigned one or two months after that. I took a couple of months off and decided to start a private practice, but I wanted to work for the practice that I dreamed of having. So I did my research, hung a shingle and put my price list out there.

I decided not to contract with insurance companies because insurance companies have kind of skewed the way that medicine is practiced. Not only are we beholden to all of their random rules and regulations, but they also recommend things or don't recommend things that are recommended. For example, there are times where as a psychiatrist, a really good therapeutic interaction is key. So sitting down and actually talking to somebody for 30 minutes is actually far more helpful than any medicine I can put them on, but insurance wouldn't pay for it. And so, I wanted to create a practice where that's not an issue, and I did that.

QUESTION: *Think about a time that you disagreed with the majority. Did you stand up for your beliefs?*

RULE #5: DON'T STOP!

There will be many times on your journey to success when you are tempted to quit. You'll want to stop. Don't do that! Don't stop! Get organized, get support, get guidance, and keep on pushing!

I could have stopped when I experienced all the poverty stuff growing up. It was really tough. I could have said, you know what, I'm going to drop out of school and get a job instead of trying to do my homework by candlelight. I could have stopped in undergrad when I got a D in chemistry because I didn't take class seriously. I could have stopped when I went through the pre-med panel and they said, with the 25 MCAT and your GPA, you probably shouldn't apply to medical school at all. I could have stopped then. And I could have stopped once I got to medical school and realized, this is so much work and they're asking a lot of me. I could have stopped in residency when I was in the throes of juggling three different residencies and I ran across an attending who hated my guts. He was so mean to me, and I could have quit then. I could have stopped once I got written up for insubordination. But I didn't because I believe in myself.

QUESTION: *What is one thing that you wanted to stop previously, but pushed through? What are your current feelings now about completing that thing?*

NOTES

DR. BRIAN H. WILLIAMS

Specialty:
Trauma Surgery

RULE #1: BE OPEN TO CHANGE.

We never know what life will throw at us and what will grab our attention. When new opportunities come, be open to change.

It wasn't my plan to become a doctor. I spent six years of active duty in the Air Force, doing research and development flight test for the Air Force, where I attained the rank of Captain. It was during that time I started getting interested in a career in medicine, but that interest was more thinking it would be a cool thing to do, but is was not for me.

I didn't go to undergrad as a pre-med; I had no concept of what it meant to get into medical school. But a lot of my social circle was in medicine, so I was continually exposed to the field. At one point, I had a discussion with one of my colleagues who had the exact background that I did, Air Force Academy graduate, an aeronautical engineer doing testing in the Air Force. He told me he was going to go to medical school.

I picked his brain for a while and realized that I did have the requirement to go to medical school.

QUESTION: *What is one thing that you are resisting change in? Why are you resisting? Is this resistance holding you back from achieving greatness?*

RULE #2: CONSIDER MONEY
WHEN MAKING DECISIONS.

People often say things like "don't worry about the money, just make the decision that's best for you." The odd things about that is money often plays a role in deciding what's best. It's typically not the most important component, but you have to consider the financial implications of your decisions.

Fortunate for me, neither decision was a bad decision. No matter what I chose, I would have ended up okay and happy. But I went to South Florida, which was financially very appealing because I could get in-state tuition. Without an exorbitant amount of money for my annual tuition, it didn't hurt my bank account too much. I still had loans I had to live off to pay the bills and buy food and things like that.

QUESTION: *What is your honest view of money? Do you view it as a tool to serve yourself, or a tool to serve others?*

RULE #3: DON'T BE SCARED TO WORK HARD.

When you work hard, you're gaining more experience. The more hours you put in, the better you'll get. Don't be scared to put in the work! It'll pay off in the end.

I had already decided that there were just a handful of iconic, busy, Urban Trauma Centers that I would consider going to for my training. The one I chose was Grady

Memorial Hospital in Atlanta, which is affiliated with Emory University and Morehouse School of Medicine. My fellowship was through Emory University and I spent two years at Grady. One year was trauma surgery. The second year was mostly in the ICU with some operating.

Grady hospital is an iconic urban trauma center, very busy as far as number of trauma activations per year. High acuity, the sickest of the sick. And that's what I wanted; to ensure that when I was done, I had seen and experienced everything that could possibly be thrown at me when I was out on my own. I knew I was going to work. I was going to live in that hospital for those two years, so I didn't miss anything.

QUESTION: *Who is the hardest working person you know? Do you think that person is happy?*

RULE #4: LET YOUR WORK ETHIC SPEAK FOR ITSELF.

We all have stereotypes; it's a human survival mechanism. Along your journey, some people will look at you and automatically assume that you won't be successful. Don't pay any attention to that. Let your work ethic speak for itself.

Stay focused on the end goal and always be at the top of your game so no one can question your abilities, qualifications or commitment. Because in the end, some will take one look at you and start making judgments about whether or not you belong, whether or not you are capable, whether or not you are truly committed. You have to erase any doubt based on your work ethic and that means being there first, staying there longer, and doing better on your test. This may seem like a lot of pressure, but this is the reality of the world in which you are entering. The standards by which you will be measured against are not the same for people who are not minorities. But that should not dissuade you from going into this profession. It should not dissuade you from just maintaining your integrity about what you're doing.

QUESTION: *Answer honestly! Are you a hard worker? If someone else was asked that question about you, what would they say?*

RULE #5: PAY IT FORWARD.

Everyone needs a little help. Someone helped you, so you should be willing to help others. Pay it forward and leave your impact on the next generation.

No matter what stage you're in, you are always in a position to pay it forward. If you're in med school now, there is a high school student to whom you can give advice. If you're a resident, you can pay it forward to a medical student, and attending and beyond, it never ends. One of the most important obligations I have is to ensure that I can always look back and say to someone who needs my help or could use my advice, "I will make time to make that happen." Many people did it for me; I didn't do this by myself. Many folks did it for me, so I want to do it for someone else.

QUESTION: *Who can you pay it forward to today?*

NOTES

DR. DARRELL M. GRAY, II

Specialty:
Gastroenterology

RULE #1: BUILD YOUR TEAM.

It's the fourth quarter with 10 seconds left on the clock, and you've got the ball. Who's on your team? If you want to be successful, you're going to need a team of individuals who are all in with you.

Medical school was tough, period. There isn't much I can compare that experience to. I had to adjust my study habits many times over. I would go from doing all-nighters to studying alone to studying in groups trying to figure out what worked best to not only understanding the sea of information but to be able to apply that information as well.

And I failed some tests, simple as that. It didn't feel good. I wasn't striving to fail. I put my best foot forward, but there were some tests that I failed. I was sure that if I failed one, I wasn't going to fail that course again or fail that test for that class again. And fortunately, I never failed any courses. But again, it was a team effort. I had some folks I was studying with who helped me to get the material. I also felt as though I had an outlet for some of the stress I was under. I could go to church, I could hang out with friends, I could call my family. It's so important to have that when you're navigating such a stressful part of your life.

QUESTION: *Who are the top three people on your personal team? Have you told them how much they mean to you and your success?*

RULE #2: REPRESENT!

*It's never just about you. Always remember that other
people are watching you, and your performance will
impact how they view other people who are like you. As a
black male doctor, I am fully aware that my performance
impacts the opportunities of those coming behind me. It's
never just about us!*

I remember an instance of the power of words while I
was in fellowship. It was a long rough day. I did some proce-
dures, I had rounded on the service, and I was doing notes,
trying to catch up. I was in a process of doing feedback on
myself, processing what I'd done that day—what I had done
wrong, what I'd done right, what I could have done better.
And I remember just kind of feeling down. As I was walk-
ing back to my area, one of the janitorial staff said, "Hey,
brother." I looked over and he smiled and said, "I'm proud
of you."

I literally stopped. His comments changed my whole
demeanor. I smiled and I said, "Thank you." It was such
a simple thing, but that had such an impact. Not only on
that day but how I proceeded on from there. I've also had
patients in the hospital or clinic who have said, "You know
what? I'm proud of you. I don't see too many African-
American brothers who are out here as a physician. I'm so
proud."

QUESTION: *Who are you representing for?*

RULE #3: APPRECIATE WHAT YOU HAVE.

People complain too much. We're always concerned about what we don't have. We often think the grass is greener on the other side, but it's not. Stop worrying about what you don't have and make the most with what you do have. Somewhere else in the world, there will likely be someone who has much less that you do.

One of my most memorable experiences during residency was when I traveled for a Global Health rotation. I traveled to Bomet, Kenya for three months at Tenwek Hospital. I remember one morning when I was managing the men's ward, the women's ward, internal medicine award, and the ICU. I was a consultant for their surgical services and occasionally staffed the emergency department as well. So it was quite busy. One morning when I was on the men's ward, I noticed a man who wasn't doing well. He was having an arrhythmia or abnormal heart rate. I called out for the crash cart, which has some medicine and different things to try to get someone out of an arrhythmia, but it didn't have what I needed. I knew what to do, I had the knowledge. But they didn't have what I needed, and I literally watched this guy die, And it was one of the most crushing feelings to see that guy's life slip away in front of me.

QUESTION: *What is one thing that you have failed to appreciate? How would your life be different if you took time to appreciate this and other "little" things?*

RULE #4: CHART YOUR OWN COURSE.

Know what works for you. People honestly want to help, but not everyone knows the best way to help you. They'll provide advice and resources that have worked for them but might not work for you. Figure out what works for you and use that to achieve greatness.

Chart your own course and don't be afraid to take risks. One of my favorite stories in the Bible is that of David and Goliath. You know the story—David was the youngest of eight sons of Jesse and a sheep herder. His three oldest brothers followed King Saul to war and were on the battlegrounds between the Israelites and the Philistines. David's father sent David to the battleground to take food to his brothers. And while doing so, he caught sight of Goliath, who was a champion of great stature and strength, challenging the Israelites. Now the Bible says that whenever the Israelites saw the man, they all fled in great fear.

However, David told Saul, "I'll fight him." King Saul offered David his coat of armor, a bronze helmet and sword. But David wisely used his own staff, picked up five smooth stones and put them in his shepherd's bag. He used his own sling and used his own tools to bring down the giant. I like that because it shows that he had some guidance. He had someone who was trying to guide him to do the right thing. But he knew what was right, he knew in his heart what tools to use, so he charted his own course and was not afraid to take a risk.

QUESTION: *Have you taken the time to write down your life's course? What risks will you have to take to accomplish your goals?*

RULE #5: **KEEP THE MAIN THING THE MAIN THING.**

Figure out what you're here to do and once you know, make that your main thing. Don't get distracted from it. The main thing needs to be the main thing!

Keep the main thing the main thing. As a student, your main job is to excel in school. You may be working outside of school, but your primary job is your education. Now on this journey, I assure you there will be distractions, and distractions can come in many forms. It can be people, places, and things. Don't be distracted; stay focused and remember you are not alone in this journey. Family and church family and friends of those who are pursuing a career in medicine, make sure that you're fostering an environment of growth. There is an intimate relationship between the environment and growth. Look at nature for examples of this. If you confine a small shark to a fish tank aquarium, it will stay the size proportionate to the space in which it is occupying. However, if you take the same shark and release it into the ocean, it will grow to its full mature size. The environment is important. Be a stimulus for people's growth. Choose your words wisely. The power of life and death lies in the tongue. Speak life into these students. Remember Jeremiah 29:11: "For I know the plans I have for you plans to prosper you and not to harm you, plans to give you hope and a future."

QUESTION: *What's your main thing?*

NOTES

SEAN BROWN

Medical Student

RULE #1: MAKE THE IMPOSSIBLE POSSIBLE.

Just because someone else thinks you can't do something doesn't mean that you can't. It probably just means they can't. If you know it's possible, simply prove them wrong.

I knew that Johns Hopkins University would be a great first step in this journey. It's a very good engineering school and a very good school for medicine. I knew it could be a good start for me. But I remember going into my college counselor's office, and we had to come up with a list of schools that I wanted to apply to. The college counselor put them into categories; the categories being possible, likely, unlikely, and nearly impossible. And Johns Hopkins was in the nearly impossible category. Without directly saying it, he discouraged me from applying to that school. And maybe it was an internal drive, but once that happened, I thought, *now I'm definitely going to apply because you think I can't do it.* I knew I could do it and that was all I needed.

I ended up applying early decision and fortunately, I got in. Going to Johns Hopkins was honestly one of the best decisions I could have made for my life.

QUESTION: *What "impossible" thing do you need to make possible? How do you plan to do that?*

RULE #2: DON'T LET THE PAST HOLD YOU BACK.

Tragedy strikes us all. When it does, it tries to hold us back and prevent us from moving forward to accomplish our

*goals. We all have darkness in our past
which we need to let go of.*

In the spring semester of my freshman year, my father passed away from pancreatic cancer he had been battling since I was in high school. Despite knowing how deadly the disease was, his constant positivity and optimism blinded me in a way. Somehow, I was convinced that he would be able to beat it, and I was shocked when he passed away. Looking back, I should have been prepared. After his death, I was emotionally all over the place. I was distraught, and it was reflected in my grades. I was depressed, feeling a lot of self-pity and self-doubt, and all those emotions compromised the drive I had. I found myself comparing myself to other people and how I didn't measure up. That extended into my sophomore year.

The summer after my sophomore year, I realized that I needed to make a transition. I attended a summer program called the Summer Medical and Dental Education program at Case Western School of Medicine, and they introduced me to the application process for medical school. With the rigor that would inevitably come with the acceptance, I realized that I needed to climb out of the valley that I was in. I needed to do it not for myself, but for my father. I made the conscious decision to leave the self-doubt that I was feeling, the pity, and the depression in the past.

QUESTION: *What is one thing in your past that has been holding you back? How do you plan to use that to move you forward?*

RULE #3: FIND THE UPSIDE!

Whether we like it or not, disappointments will come. When they do, our initial reaction is to complain and see the glass as half empty. But remember this, there's always an upside to the situation. Find that upside!

I chose Temple to pursue my dream of becoming a doctor.

After deciding, I got a call from the office of diversity stating that I was the only African American male in my class, and at first I was kind of upset. I thought, *Come on, man.* I chose Temple because the community that we served was mostly made up of African American and Latino people, but also the student body was pretty diverse. A good amount of African Americans go there. But after some reflection, I realized that I was fortunate to be able to represent such a significant and vulnerable population in the United States. I try to remind myself that because it can be a little demoralizing in situations where you're the only black kid in the class.

QUESTION: *What is the first "disappointing" thing in your life that comes to mind? What is the upside to that thing?*

RULE #4: TURN YOUR LEMONS INTO LEMONADE.

Every negative situation is an opportunity for greatness. Figure out how to make the most out of challenging times!

I got my first interview in September and I was hyped.

A few days later, though, adversity kept coming in my life. I tore my ACL, I tore my lateral meniscus and I had a bone bruise. I was playing basketball at the time and I thought, *Really? Why is this happening?* I could not catch a break. At all of my interviews, I was either on crutches, in a big brace or both, but I knew I could not let this stop me. I honestly used this to my advantage; I used it as a talking point in many of my interviews. I am truly blessed to say that I received eight acceptances, two which gave me a full ride.

QUESTION: *Do you remember the "disappointing" thing from Rule #4? Are you ready to make lemonade today?*

RULE #5: STAY THE COURSE.
People will try to knock you off track and discourage you. Don't let them do that. Stay on track!

Don't let anyone discourage you from doing what you want to do. This is your life. There will always be obstacles in your life, but remember, once you find your passion stay on course. Don't let anyone or anything get in the way of that. Just remember to stay on course.

QUESTION: *What is one way people are trying to knock you off track right now? What can you do to prevent them from doing that?*

NOTES

DR. JASON CAMPBELL

Specialty:
Anesthesiology

RULE #1: BE THE SPARKPLUG–
DON'T WAIT FOR OTHERS TO ACT.

Leaders tend to be self-starters. When they see a problem, they want to fix it. It's easy to hope someone else will take on the task, but that often leads to nothing happening. Be the sparkplug!

My mother, Lucile L Adams Campbell, was the first African American female to get a Ph.D. in epidemiology in the country. When people ask her, "What was your impetus? What was your reason for doing the research in minority health?" She was a black girl who grew up in southeast Washington, DC, in the hood. She saw a gap and saw no one doing anything about it and realized that she needed to do something about it. There was a deficiency and she wanted to fix it because she wasn't going leave it up to somebody else. And that's what this whole minority in medicine, black men in medicine is about; there's a deficiency. There is a gap between the numbers of black men in medicine versus white men in medicine versus other races and ethnicities. We are the ones that we've been waiting for. We're saying hey, we're here to fix this. We're here to help combat this issue because we know diversity saves lives. We know that together we're stronger. We know that we can make a difference, but we have to make it individually first.

QUESTION: *What is one thing that you believe needs to be done right now in your community? Can you be the sparkplug to get it started?*

RULE #2: DO WHAT YOU NEED TO DO TODAY, SO YOU CAN DO WHAT YOU WANT TO DO TOMORROW.

We want instant gratification, but often, great rewards don't come that way. Sacrifice is hard, however, if you're willing to do it now, you can reap the benefits later.

Realize that every day matters. Are you doing what you need to do today so you can do what you want tomorrow? When you're in Manassas, Virginia, on Sully Road in a Starbucks at 11 p.m. on a Friday night, with your MCAT book open, I know that can feel lonely, but I've been there, and others have been there. I experienced that firsthand. But sometimes that anonymity, being closed off from the world to pursue your dreams and your passions, is such an exciting time because not only are you studying, but you're also reflecting. And all that reflection and introspection is going to make you a better physician, a better researcher, a better scientist.

QUESTION: *What should you be doing today? Are you doing it?*

RULE #3: GET BACK ON YOUR HORSE!

If you don't ever get knocked off your horse, you're probably not going after anything worthwhile. So, when you do get knocked off, don't stay down. Get back up and keep going.

I got a phone call that said I did not pass. Talk about devastating. This was something that was going to potentially change my future. Would I still graduate on time in four years? Was I still going to be able to apply to general surgery? Would I be able to go do that away rotation at Wayne State at the DMC? Would I go to that away rotation at Hopkins? A lot of things are going through my head. And for the first 24 hours, I was worried and concerned. After 24 hours, I had to do something about it.

I had to get back on the horse and start studying again. I had to reconfigure those away rotations. Thankfully, God is good. I was able to set all that stuff up so I didn't miss a beat. But believe me, there was some angst and anxiety associated with that time, but look at me now, right? We all go through things, and it's part of the journey. It's part of this journey in medicine, it is part of this journey as a minority in medicine, and it's certainly part of this journey as a black man in medicine.

I re-studied for the exam, was able to pass the second time by a very small number. I always think about how our journeys go. Robert Frost said that two paths diverged in the woods, and I took the lesser path. That's the reason that I am the man I am today.

QUESTION: *What horse have you been knocked off recently? Are you ready to get back on it?*

RULE #4: ASK FOR HELP.

*Pride can be our biggest downfall. We are ashamed to admit
we need help at times. Over the years, I've come to learn that
some of the most successful people I know don't have this
problem. They ask for help when they need it.
You should do the same.*

Inevitably, it's all about priming ourselves and getting
ourselves ready for the hurdles that we will face by asking
for help.

Why is asking for help frowned upon? Why do our people find it so difficult to ask for help? Maybe because we're
worried about looking weak or people perceiving us as less
than them. I'll tell you one thing, if you don't ask for help,
you may not look weak, but inevitably if you don't get to
where you want to go, who loses in the end? You do. All
of my successes that I have obtained to this point are due
to asking for help. I asked for help when I was an undergrad. I asked for help when I was in my master's program.
I asked for help when I was in medical school. I asked for
help as a resident; as an attendee, I'll ask for help. One day
if I'm so lucky to be program director or chair, I'm going to
ask others for help to make sure that my program, that my
department, is running smoothly.

But that's a common theme. We don't want to ask for
help and we need to stop that! Ask for help. And when others ask you for help, help them.

QUESTION: *What is one thing you need help with? Who can
you ask to help you? Ask!*

RULE #5: PREPARE TO PERSEVERE.

*The road to success is a long one and at times you'll likely
want to quit...but don't! Rather, prepare to persevere.
Hold on to the good times because you'll need them to get
through the tough ones.*

I was in the Portland Veteran Affairs Hospital and a tall
African-American gentleman was sitting on the stretcher
on the gurney. I walked and said, "Hi, I'm Dr. Campbell.
Please call me Jason."

He looked at me and said, "I am so glad to see you." I
never forget times like that. It makes all of it worth it and
makes all the hardship, frustration, sadness, emptiness,
headaches, and heartaches worth it. Be ready for perse-
verance. Tuck that in your pocket, because you're going to
need it. Know you're going to face some hardships but it'll
be worth it.

When my coach says, "If it was easy, everyone would
do it," I know that it's a special calling. I don't want to say
career, it's a *calling*. Because I feel like there's no way with
the adversity that I faced that it could be anything less than
a calling to be here, right now.

QUESTION: *What is one way in which you are preparing yourself to persevere?*

NOTES

_____

_____

_____

_____

_____

_____

_____

_____

_____

_____

_____

_____

_____

_____

_____

_____

_____

_____

_____

_____

_____

DR. CLARENCE LEE JR.

Specialty:
Occupational Medicine

RULE #1: DEVELOP YOUR INTERPERSONAL SKILLS.

Credentials matter, but what matters even more is whether or not people like you. Learn how to earn people's trust and respect.

When you ask other people questions and you find similarities between you and the other person, it's very, very easy to make friends. This is really, really important, especially for minorities. If you're going into medicine or you're going into a field where you might be one of the few, interpersonal skills are massively important. And I think one of the things that helped me the most was that I was able to relate to people; I was able to make friends with people.

When people like you, they look out for you, they take care of you, and they do nice things for you. You get invited to parties, and you're everybody's friend. When you are people's friend, it makes things a lot easier for you. So while a lot of people look at credentials, and GPAs, all that stuff is important. But, speaking from my heart, what has been valuable to me is interpersonal skills. I learned interpersonal skills by being the new kid. Try to find similarities between you and others. Make strategic alliances, people that you know you need on your team. Understand how to ask them questions about themselves. Be genuinely interested in other people. As you navigate through life, that's going to pay massive dividends for you.

QUESTION: *On a scale of 0-10, how strong are your interpersonal skills? What can you do to strengthen them?*

RULE #2: LEARN FROM HISTORY'S GREAT LEADERS.

Our potential does not have to be limited to that of the people in our environment. If you are not satisfied with the role models in your community, pick up a book and read about one who satisfies you.

The reason I love Black History Month is because I see a different option for myself. I see the truth about the type of people I came from, the quality of individuals, and how educated we are. The things we've been able to do in life and in the history of the world, the contributions that the Africans and African-Americans have been able to make. I learned that from books. Instead of looking on TV and listening to songs, I decided to go to Black History Month to figure out who I was. And it showed me that there were a lot of opportunities for me.

Learn your history. History is important because it shapes identity. For me, history gave me a different look for who I was. I believed that I was a scientist because I read about black scientist. I believed I could be a doctor because I read about black doctors. I started a tradition of the Black History Month program in the fifth grade and put the whole program together. I think it was an awesome, awesome thing for that school. In the beginning, it was books because I didn't have the role models in my neighborhood. So my role models were virtual role models, and that's how my eyes started to become open to what was truly possible for me.

QUESTION: *Who do you believe is the greatest leader to walk the planet? Why? What is one thing you can take from that person's leadership style?*

RULE #3: READ, READ, READ!

*Leaders tend to be readers. Just think about how
a book is made: an author sits down and takes the time to
gather the best information he or she can to put into one
book. Take this book for example—I've spent a long time
making sure it's worth your while to read. By reading, you're
giving yourself an advantage!*

I did well in school because I love to learn. I loved reading, and I don't know why but that was my thing. I liked learning new stuff. I loved challenges. I got excited if the teacher told me I couldn't do a hundred math problems. I'd think, *oh you think I can't? Okay, I'm going show you.* That was just the type of kid I was. So a lot of people ask me why I was that type of kid. I don't know. I can't really answer that but I know I loved to learn.

School was fun for me, and school was a challenge for me. I wanted to show everyone that just because I was black, that didn't mean that I had to do poorly, and that did not mean I wasn't capable of doing well in a classroom. I always wanted to do well, and I did well.

QUESTION: *What three books will you read next?*

RULE #4: CHOOSE YOUR ENVIRONMENT.

*This one is tough because it's not easy for people to up and
leave an area because they don't like it. That being said,
sometimes, in order to succeed, you have to find a way to do
just that. Ultimately, you must choose the right environment.*

My time at East High School was very life-changing and life-forming. It was in Binghampton, which is a tough part of Memphis. It was a rough school. At the end of my second year there, one of my friends was shot and killed at school. This was a really critical moment for me. I knew that if I stayed in environment that I was in—guns and drugs every day at school, during basketball kids pulling guns out so they could play, marijuana everywhere—It wouldn't be good for me. I told my mom, "Hey, you're going to have to get me out of this school or something bad is gonna happen." I didn't know what that meant, I just knew that it wasn't a good place for me. And I knew I needed to be somewhere else.

I convinced my mom to take me down to the school board. I told to the president of the school board: "I need to get out of this school. Look at my grades, I'm a good student. I want to be able to go to one of the nicer public schools." At the time, it was a minority to majority transfer. I joined what's called the Optional Program, which is where you took honors classes. It was by the grace of God, and I'm a man of faith, that the school board principal heard me and my mom and let me transfer out of that school.

QUESTION: *Are you happy with your current environment? What is one thing you can do to make your environment better?*

RULE #5: FIGHT FOR YOUR VISION.

If you want your vision to come to fruition,
you have to go after it. It's your vision and your
responsibility. At times, you'll have to break away
from the norm and be the odd ball in the group.
It takes courage to be successful.

One of the things I learned was time management. I was the only biology major on the basketball team. With biology, I had to do labs in undergrad, and I had to negotiate with my teammates in college because I had to miss certain film times during the day because I had to go to my lab. The moral of that story is sometimes, you got to fight for what you want. You got to fight for your vision, and you got to be willing to speak up for yourself when it's needed. For me, I had to speak up to my teammates and say, "Hey, I got a lab, it's from two to three and I know that's our normal film time. So I'm going to miss some film time, but I'll make it up and I'll make up the weights time and I'll do extra."

QUESTION: *What is your life vision statement? Have you written it down?*

NOTES

DR. MAURICE SHOLAS

Specialty:
Physical Medicine & Rehabilitation

RULE #1: BE A TRAILBLAZER!

Someone has to be the first. Why not you?

I don't recall going to a specific doctor growing up. We went to the clinic and just saw whoever was available. I'm not sure where my connection to medicine started, but I knew I wanted to be a doctor ever since I was six. I don't have any close relatives who are physicians, but I do have a distant cousin who is a dentist. You don't have to come from a long line of doctors and know how everything is supposed to be upfront to be successful in your journey. It's okay to walk into things and be a trailblazer and a first-timer and really, really use your network and your skills and process to find your way through, whereas other people might have had a map.

QUESTION: *What is one thing that you can step up in, and lead with innovation?*

RULE #2: FIND THE OPPORTUNITY IN EVERY DISAPPOINTMENT.

When one door closes, another one opens for you.
Don't spend too much time stressing about the
disappointment. Instead, look for the opportunity.

In high school I experienced disappointment. Something I really wanted to work out just didn't. It was a small thing but at the time, at that age, everything feels like it's the end of the Earth. I tried out for a play and thought that the lead role was destined and written for me, but I did not get that role. I couldn't believe it, I couldn't understand it; I thought I sang better than the other people, I thought I was a stronger performer, but alas, the director of the show didn't agree and I didn't get the part.

From that disillusionment and loss, I discovered the individual speaking events of forensics and public speaking. That's something I went on to do and ultimately became a national champion in. My point of that story is, I never would have known that I was a good individual speaker or a good interpreter of material had I not experienced that initial disappointment. So, whenever your disappointment happens or whatever thing you really thought was for you and didn't work out, usually those are learning opportunities to figure out actually where you're supposed to be and what you're supposed to be doing. I'm living testimony to that.

QUESTION: *What is one opportunity that you are overlooking because you view it as a disappointment?*

RULE #3: KEEP IT SIMPLE AND DON'T OVERTHINK.

Most of life's decisions can be made based on your gut instinct. At times, however, we get caught up in the details and add unnecessary variables to the equation. Don't do that—just keep it simple.

The downside is that I had a certain amount of ignorance going into the medical application process, but the upside is that I didn't know enough to psych myself out and be terrified and afraid. For example, I thought that if you turned in your application on time and paid the application money that they gave you an interview to med school. I didn't know enough to know that there was a level of discernment and a level of exclusion that happens between the applicants and people that move on to the interview process. For me, that was a good thing because had I known I might have over thought it and put myself into a bond. In going through this process, knowledge, information and perspective is important, but it's also important not to overthink things to the point where you do yourself a disservice.

QUESTION: *What is one thing that you are overthinking? How can you simplify that thing?*

RULE #4: BUILD A VILLAGE OF PEOPLE WHO WANT TO SEE YOU SUCCEED.

This point is critical. A lot of us say that we have mentors and advisors, however, not all of those mentors and advisors are truly vested in our success. How would your mentor feel if you didn't succeed? Would they shrug it off, or would they be heartbroken? Find the ones who would be heartbroken.

Relationships matter. When you are a black man trying to get somewhere in a rare field, people you know, people that care for you, people that want to see you succeed are your greatest assets. If it hadn't been for Dr. Carlos Vital, a black man in a white coat practicing Allergy and Immunology in Houston, asking me if I was interested in coming home and following that up by talking to the gentleman that was the section chief for Physical Medicine and Rehab at LSU. If he hadn't made that connection personally, the trajectory of my career would be different. So thank you, Dr. Vital. You can be brilliant, you can be great, you can be accomplished and you can be well-versed, but you need your village and community to help you translate that into what you want to happen.

QUESTION: *Who are the five people in your life that want you to succeed the most? How can you find five more people like them?*

RULE #5: DREAM BIG!

You never know what God has planned for you,
so don't limit yourself. You have great potential therefore
you should always dream big!

When I started this journey at six years old, I didn't know that I'd be an MD, PhD from Harvard, with experience as a senior medical executive, not just shaping lives one patient interaction at a time or one family at a time, but one hospital system at a time.

You don't know, so never be afraid to dream big! Never be afraid to walk a path nobody's ever heard of, and never be afraid to lean on your village because they are your biggest cheerleaders and your biggest support system.

QUESTION: *What is your current dream? How can you make that dream even bigger?*

NOTES

_____

_____

_____

_____

_____

_____

_____

_____

_____

_____

_____

_____

_____

_____

_____

_____

_____

_____

_____

SHOWLY NICHOLSON

Medical Student

RULE #1: **LEARN FROM THE LITTLE THINGS.**

Everything in life is significant. You can learn from anything. Find every opportunity to learn, even from the little things.

I remember one particular day when I was in third grade, we had a coloring assignment for homework. We had to color the pigs and the cows and whatnot. I was at the kitchen table, and my dad looked over my shoulder and he noticed that I was coloring outside the lines; I was scribbling. He said: "Son, let me show you how to do this."

He took the crayon and he outlined the animal very neatly in a dark color and then he shaded the inside a lighter color. "That's how you color neatly. That's how you do a good job." That was the first moment I realized that school was something that you wanted to do very well in. School is something that you want to do your best at and continue to improve at and get good marks in and to learn for your own future.

And that one moment of my dad telling me how to properly color, plus he taught me how to read, how to write well, how to speak well, how to participate, all these things were very, very important for me and my future. That was the first moment I really made it a priority to do well in school and to listen to the teacher and learn.

QUESTION: *What is one "little" thing that you can learn from today?*

RULE #2: LEARN FROM GREATNESS.

So many wonderful people have done amazing things before us. No matter what field they are in, you can always learn from greatness.

The oldest standing wooden structure in the world, Horyuji Temple, was built in 700 AD. It is still standing today. Of course, it's been renovated a little bit and touched up, but a lot of the wood is built like it was originally and that's because of the way it was made.

I was fascinated about that and so I apprenticed at the Museum. I did a lot of translation work; I was around tools and carpenters. I watched and learned how they worked and how it's a lifestyle for them. The way they lived, the way they ate, the way they spoke, they were very humble; it was a type of being that influenced the quality of work that they did, and that really inspired me.

At the time, I was on the fence about pursuing medicine. I was interested in it, I wanted to help people, I liked the science and the academic rigor of it, but I didn't know if I wanted to really commit to the lifetime of schooling and development that it takes, the long road that it is. And when I realized that these carpenters were doing things that aren't supposed to be possible, like building wooden buildings that lasted thousands of years because of the lifestyle that they had, that ultimately inspired me to continue with medicine because I was excited about what I could achieve by living the principles of the traditional Japanese carpenter.

QUESTION: *What would you consider to be mankind's great-*

est accomplishment? What three things can you learn from that accomplishment?

RULE #3: DON'T WAIT, BE PROACTIVE.

Too often we wait for people to approach us with the answers we want. The problem with that is other people might want the same thing, but may not be waiting. If that's the case, you could end up waiting for something that's already been given away. Go and get whatever it is you desire.

I woke up at 3 a.m. and I started crying because I was so exhausted, but I knew what I had to do—I had to pursue getting off the waitlist at Harvard Medical School and do whatever it took until they told me no. And as much as I was tired, as much as I could choose to lay back and move away and go to another school, I gave it my all and said, "You know what, I'm going to do this. I'm going to go for this."

So I went for it. I talked to as many people as I could to learn more ways that I could still be a strong prospect to get off the waiting list. I wrote update letters, I spoke with my mentors and so on and so forth, and I ended up getting off and getting into Harvard Medical School. I still remember the email that came in one morning when I was working in research that said, "Congratulations, you are accepted." I slept really well that night. That was probably ten years of not sleeping enough, all made up for in the deepest sleep I've ever had after getting into Harvard Medical School.

QUESTION: *What is one thing that you have been waiting to do? What action can you take today to get it started?*

RULE #4: BE RESOURCEFUL AND EXECUTE!

In the age of digital media, lack of resources is no longer a valid excuse. In a matter of minutes, we can get answers to all sorts of questions. Successful people know how to find and utilize resources.

If I could boil down my whole education at Harvard University undergraduate into two things, it would first, be resourceful.

The world is full of resources to use! We can read books, listen to podcasts, speak with other people who are successful, and get their best advice. We can talk to teachers, professors, use our senses to touch things, smell things, see things. We can use our motor neurons to help emulate what we would like to achieve, the things that you like and we see in other people, to be resourceful, to develop yourself.

The second most important thing I learned at Harvard is to execute. We must use all the things we learn and act on them; use your hands and really take action in pursuit of what you would like to achieve.

QUESTION: *What is one resource that you have access to which you have not taken advantage of? How can you begin taking advantage of that resource today?*

RULE #5: **HOLD ON TO YOUR DREAMS.**

Sometimes, when things don't go our way, we begin to doubt ourselves and question our dreams. It is critical that we remain convicted in our dreams and hold on to them!

Dream and hold on to those dreams. My favorite movie is *Pursuit of Happyness* with Will Smith, because of his pursuit of his dream of becoming something great. He was homeless and had a son to care for, but he pursued his dream, and he became! I hold onto that. In the movie, he tells his son to hold onto your dreams because people tell you, you can't do something because they can't do it themselves. And I think that couldn't be truer and that's been true in my life as well. So, the first thing I want to say is to dream, and the next thing is to believe in those dreams and to believe in yourself.

QUESTION: *What one thing is trying to pull your dreams away from you? What can you do to pull your dreams closer?*

NOTES

THE FINAL CHALLENGE!

This book is about growth! Throughout our journey together, I have challenged you on a daily basis to take action in order to implement the rules of success that lie within these pages. I have no doubt that you are a stronger individual today than you were 100 days ago. Because that is the case, I'd like to leave you with two last challenges.

CHALLENGE #1: Finish writing this book! I want you to finish writing my book for me. The last chapter is all yours! Based on your own life experiences, what are your five rules for success? Shoot me an email with your photo and your five rules.
Rules@BlackMenInWhiteCoats.org.

CHALLENGE #2: Pay it forward! My hope is that the people I help will go on to help others. The true measure of success is how much you do for others. Don't grow in vain. Develop as a person so that you can help others!

MY PRAYER FOR YOU!

My prayer for you is that this book has opened your mind to a new and brighter way of thinking. I pray that you have been challenged beyond your wildest dreams and that you have come to a realization of the greatness that lies within you through the power of Christ Jesus. I pray for your family, I pray for your friends, and to my future clinicians, I pray for your patients. May the good Lord grant you innumerable blessings. In the mighty name of Jesus, I pray. Amen.

YOUR CHAPTER

YOUR NAME HERE

Speciality

RULE #1:

RULE #2:

RULE #3:

RULE #4:

RULE #5:

*Join Our Online Community of Diverse
Premeds, Medical Students, & Doctors at:*

www.DiverseMedicine.com

Make sure you
do this!

Other Books By Dr. Dale

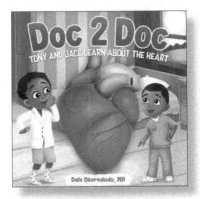